GEOLOGY ROCKS!

DISCOVER ROCKS

CHRISTINE PETERSEN

Checkerboard
Library

An Imprint of Abdo Publishing
abdobooks.com

ABDOBOOKS.COM

Published by Abdo Publishing, a division of ABDO, PO Box 398166, Minneapolis, Minnesota 55439.
Copyright © 2020 by Abdo Consulting Group, Inc. International copyrights reserved in all countries.
No part of this book may be reproduced in any form without written permission from the publisher.
Checkerboard Library™ is a trademark and logo of Abdo Publishing.

Printed in the United States of America, North Mankato, Minnesota
102019
012020

THIS BOOK CONTAINS
RECYCLED MATERIALS

Design: Emily O'Malley, Mighty Media, Inc.
Production: Mighty Media, Inc.
Editor: Jessica Rusick
Cover Photograph: Shutterstock Images
Interior Photographs: Library of Congress, p. 4; Mighty Media, Inc., pp. 26, 27; Niels Stensen/Wikimedia Commons, p. 6; Shutterstock Images, pp. 5, 7, 8, 9, 11, 13, 15, 16, 17, 19, 21, 24, 25, 29; SPENCER SUTTON/SCIENCE SOURCE, pp. 22, 23; TED M. KINSMAN/SCIENCE SOURCE, p. 12

Library of Congress Control Number: 2019943212

Publisher's Cataloging-in-Publication Data
Names: Petersen, Christine, author.
Title: Discover rocks / by Christine Petersen
Description: Minneapolis, Minnesota : Abdo Publishing, 2020 | Series: Geology rocks! | Includes online resources and index.
Identifiers: ISBN 9781532191718 (lib. bdg.) | ISBN 9781532178443 (ebook)
Subjects: LCSH: Geology--Juvenile literature. | Rocks--Juvenile literature. | Rocks--Classification--Juvenile literature. | Mineralogy--Juvenile literature.
Classification: DDC 552--dc23

CONTENTS

EXPLORING THE GRAND CANYON

In spring 1869, ten men stepped into four small boats. The men were headed down the Green River toward the Colorado River. The journey would take them through Wyoming, Colorado, Utah, and Arizona. Most importantly, it would take them through a giant canyon. No one had ever completed this dangerous journey.

Major John Wesley Powell led this brave team. The men faced many challenges. The boats were tossed and turned through rocky **rapids**. The raging water destroyed one boat. Three of the men quit before the trip ended.

Along with these challenges, the explorers saw many wonders. In some places, the canyon walls rose up an entire mile (2 km). In his journal, Powell described the amazing colors of the canyon's rock layers. They glowed in shades of gray, white, pink, purple, and more.

Major John Wesley Powell

4

The Grand Canyon is about 277 miles (446 km) long.
It is located in Arizona.

After three months, Powell and his remaining team members safely completed their journey. They breathed a sigh of relief. Yet, Powell was eager to return to what he named the Grand Canyon. He soon began planning his next trip through this amazing rock formation.

LAYERS OF ROCK

Powell wanted more than adventure on his daring trips. Powell was a geologist. He saw evidence of the planet's history in the Grand Canyon's rock layers.

Most rock forms in layers, which are called strata. In the 1660s, scientist Nicolaus Steno made important observations about this process. Steno decided that lower layers must form first. Upper layers form later in time on top of older ones. This is called the law of superposition.

The effect is similar to making a layer cake. The first layer of cake is placed on a plate. Then, it is covered with icing. Another layer of cake goes on top of that, followed by more icing. No matter how many layers are added, the

Nicolaus Steno

Steno stated that strata form evenly with the horizon. If they look tilted or folded, this happened after the rock formed.

bottom one will have been on the plate longest. That is because it was put down first.

This layering effect is easy to see in the Grand Canyon. More than 40 rock strata have been identified there. The flowing Colorado River exposes the oldest layers at the bottom. Rocks high up at the rim of the canyon are much younger.

WHAT IS ROCK?

Over time, geologists have learned what rock is. Rock forms the solid part of Earth's crust. Rocks are not living things. Instead, they are made of minerals.

Minerals are solid substances that occur naturally. They are formed from chemical **elements**. These elements are made of tiny building blocks called atoms.

Most minerals contain two or more elements. Their atoms fit together to produce a repeating pattern. Every mineral has its own pattern. Scientists have identified more than 4,000 minerals.

Like ingredients in a recipe, minerals combine to produce different types of rock. A type of rock called limestone is made mostly of the mineral calcite. Most rocks contain more than one

Egypt's Great Sphinx was carved from limestone.

Mount Rushmore National Memorial in South Dakota was carved from granite.

type of mineral. For example, granite contains the minerals quartz and feldspar. It also contains smaller amounts of several other minerals.

BENEATH
OUR FEET

If Earth were sliced in half, you would see that it has several layers. Like a peach pit, Earth's core lies at its center. This hot ball is packed with the **elements** iron and nickel. The inner core is solid. The outer core is liquid.

Earth's next layer is called the mantle. It makes up more than 80 percent of Earth's volume. The mantle is solid. But, its rock is very hot. So, it can flow slowly, like a glacier creeping down a valley.

Like a peach's skin, Earth's outer layer is thin. This rock layer is called the crust. It covers every part of the planet, from the seafloor to the mountaintops.

Yet Earth's crust is not a single piece of rock. Instead, it is broken into huge pieces called tectonic plates. Earth's crust is made up of about 15 to 20 tectonic plates. They fit together like jigsaw puzzle pieces.

However, Earth's puzzle is never finished. Heat from the mantle causes the plates to pull and push in new directions. The plates **collide**, separate, and slide past one another. These movements can produce new rock.

EARTH'S LAYERS

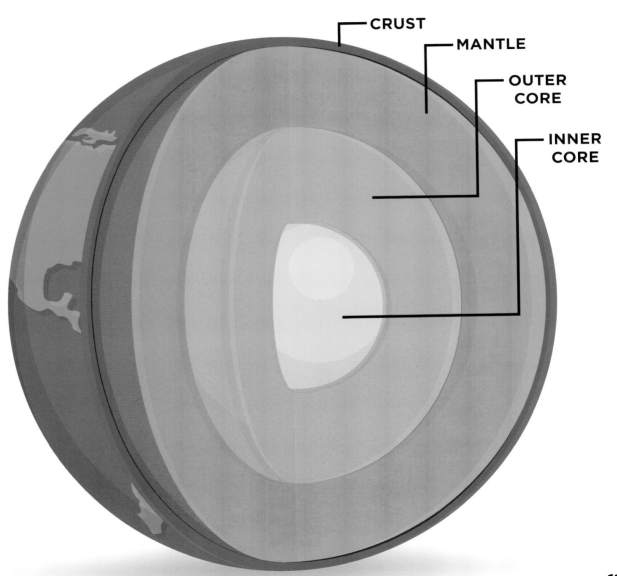

CRUST

MANTLE

OUTER CORE

INNER CORE

MADE FROM FIRE

Scientists divide rock into three types based on how it forms. These are igneous, sedimentary, and metamorphic rock. The most common is igneous rock. It forms as **magma** cools and hardens.

Magma forms beneath or within Earth's crust. Then, it flows upward. When it erupts at the surface, it is called lava. Lava cools quickly to form rock. Igneous rock produced this way is called extrusive or volcanic rock.

Most volcanoes form where tectonic plates move apart or push together. Others form above areas called **hot spots**. In either case, pressure builds inside or below a volcano and must be released. Whoosh! The magma bursts upward.

The island of Hawaii is home to one of the most active volcanoes on Earth.

Pumice will float on water.

Lava flowing from Kilauea and cooling

Kilauea has erupted continuously since January 1983. These eruptions can be violent and send lava high into the sky. Or, the lava can emerge like a slow, orange river. The lava cools and hardens to form new rock.

New rock from a volcano may look like wrinkled black fabric. Other lava cools so quickly it forms a lightweight igneous rock called pumice. It has holes from gases that escaped as the lava cooled. Volcanoes are amazing natural wonders. They let us see brand new rock!

DEVILS TOWER

Sometimes, **magma** stops rising before it reaches Earth's surface. It cools and hardens underground. This can take thousands or even millions of years. Igneous rock that forms this way is called intrusive or plutonic rock.

Magma that forms this rock may cool between older rock strata. Or, it may cut across several rock layers. It may also push rock up from below to form a dome shape.

Devils Tower in Wyoming is a stunning example of intrusive rock. The tower rises high above the flat surrounding land. Hike close to Devils Tower and you will see its most interesting feature. It is made up of huge, vertical rock columns.

BEAR CLAWS!

Devils Tower is a sacred landmark to local Native American tribes. They have stories that explain how it formed. These include tales of people running away from bears. The people ran to a low rock, which then grew higher into the sky. As the bears tried to climb the new tower, their powerful claws scratched it. This created the deep marks we see in the rock today.

Devils Tower rises 867 feet (264 m) from its wide base to its flat top. The tower is popular with rock climbers.

Geologists believe the tower began forming more than 50 million years ago. **Magma** rose up, but it was held below Earth's surface rocks. Slowly, the magma formed rock that shrank as it cooled. This produced the columns we see today.

This new intrusive rock was harder than the rock surrounding it. Over time, water wore away those older rocks. The tower remained and was slowly exposed.

THE ROCK CYCLE

Igneous rock forms as **magma** cools above or below Earth's surface.

Magma

Wind, rain, and ice break down and move rock to new places. There, the rock fragments are pressed together to form layers of sedimentary rock.

Metamorphic rock forms when heat or pressure changes igneous or sedimentary rock. Extreme heat turns metamorphic rock into **magma**.

BREAKING
DOWN ROCK

Rocks are strong. Yet they age and change just like people do. Wind, water, and ice are forces that lead to **weathering** and erosion. These processes cause rocks to break down and change.

When weathering occurs, the rock remains in its original position. Erosion is a similar process. But it moves bits of rock away from their original location.

Water and ice can be especially powerful. Water can seep into cracks and wash away parts of the rock. When water freezes, it expands. This widens the cracks, and bits of rock may eventually break off.

Utah's Arches National Park has experienced these changes. There, water and ice have carved the sandstone rock. Today, the park contains elegant arches and other beautiful rock formations.

Certain acids can form in water. These acids can **dissolve** rock such as limestone and marble. Over time, small holes grow into massive caves. Mammoth Cave in Kentucky was formed by this process. It is the longest known cave system in the world!

There are more than 2,000 arches in Arches National Park. Some are very small. Others are more than 306 feet (93 m) across!

Living things also help rocks break down. Plants may grow in cracks in rocks. Their tiny roots are strong! They push against the rock, which widens the cracks. Eventually, the rock breaks apart.

OLD ROCKS
TO NEW ROCKS

Great mountains slowly crumble under the effects of **weathering** and erosion. Pebbles, sand, and **silt** may roll down mountains and valleys. Some of these sediments are even small enough to be carried by the wind.

Many sediments fall into lakes, rivers, and oceans. The sediments settle to the bottom, layer by layer. Over time, the weight of new layers pushes together the layers below.

At the same time, water trickling through the sediments leaves behind minerals. These minerals act like glue and cement everything together. This creates sedimentary rock.

Many strata in the Grand Canyon are sedimentary. There are colorful layers of sandstone, limestone, and shale. These formed when water covered the area at various times long ago.

Different substances combined to form the various types of sedimentary rock. Sandstone forms from sand-sized grains of rocks and minerals. Limestone is made from the shells and bones of ancient sea animals. Shale forms from clay.

Water helped create the Grand Canyon's sedimentary layers. Then, the Colorado River carved out the canyon to reveal those layers!

After these layers formed, tectonic plates **collided**. Between 70 and 30 million years ago, this plate collision made the land rise. And over time, the Colorado River carved out the Grand Canyon.

GEOLOGIC TIME SCALE

The geologic time scale is like a calendar of Earth's history. Instead of years, months, and days, scientists organize time into other groups. Eons last the longest. Eras are next, followed by periods. Epochs come next. Ages last the shortest amount of time. The different groups are based on Earth's rock layers and the fossils they contain.

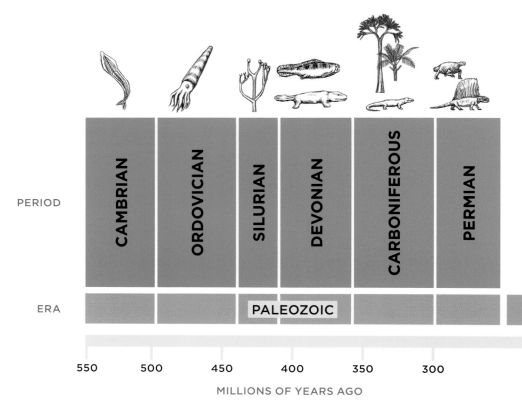

	CAMBRIAN	ORDOVICIAN	SILURIAN	DEVONIAN	CARBONIFEROUS	PERMIAN
PERIOD						
ERA			PALEOZOIC			

550   500   450   400   350   300

MILLIONS OF YEARS AGO

Different types of life appear at different times on the geologic time scale. The first fish arrived in the Cambrian period, followed by amphibians in the Devonian period. Next, reptiles appeared in the Carboniferous period. The Triassic period had the first dinosaurs and the first mammals. Birds arrived during the Jurassic period. The Cretaceous period saw the first primates. Finally, humans appeared in the Quaternary period of the geologic time scale.

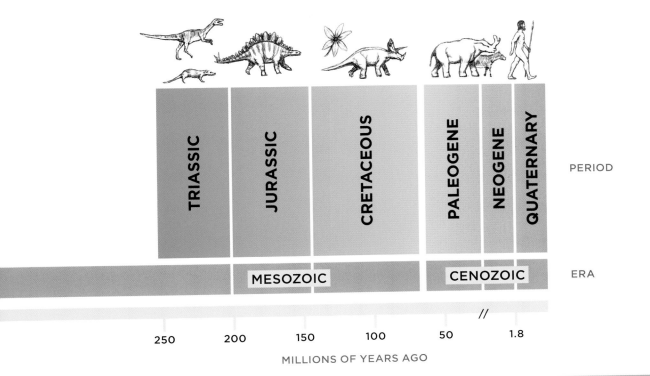

PERIOD						
TRIASSIC	JURASSIC	CRETACEOUS	PALEOGENE	NEOGENE	QUATERNARY	

MESOZOIC   CENOZOIC   ERA

//

250   200   150   100   50   1.8

MILLIONS OF YEARS AGO

CHANGING FORM

The third type of rock is metamorphic rock. It forms from igneous or sedimentary rock. Great heat and pressure can cause minerals within existing rocks to change shape and size. These forces may even rearrange atoms completely to form new minerals. Different minerals make different types of rocks.

Limestone is a sedimentary rock. However, heat and pressure can transform it into marble. Marble is a valuable metamorphic rock used for sculptures.

The motion of tectonic plates creates tremendous pressure on rocks. They are squashed, twisted, and heated, which turns them into new forms. This kind of change has happened along the coast of California. There, old rock

Serpentinite

Slate is a type of metamorphic rock. It is used
to make floors, roofs, and blackboards.

changed into a new metamorphic rock called serpentinite.
This glossy, colorful rock is the California state rock.

Sometimes, one tectonic plate slides under another. The
lower plate is forced down into Earth's mantle. The rock
melts into **magma**. Later, this may form new igneous rock.
This is part of the rock cycle.

TRY THIS AT HOME:
MAKE METAMORPHIC ROCK!

WHAT YOU'LL NEED

+ modeling clay in at least 3 colors
+ 2 sheets of waxed paper
+ several heavy books
+ knife (optional)

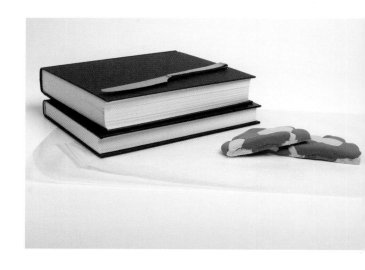

WHAT YOU'LL DO

1. Make about ten small balls from each color of clay. The balls represent rocks.

2. Mix up the colors and pile the balls on one piece of waxed paper.

3. Place the other piece of waxed paper on top of the pile.

4. Stack the books on top of the waxed paper. Press down on the books to flatten the clay balls.

5. Remove the books and pull off the top piece of waxed paper.

6. Break or cut the clay in half. Do you see how it has changed? Pressure from the books created a new piece of clay. This is similar to how old rock becomes new metamorphic rock within Earth!

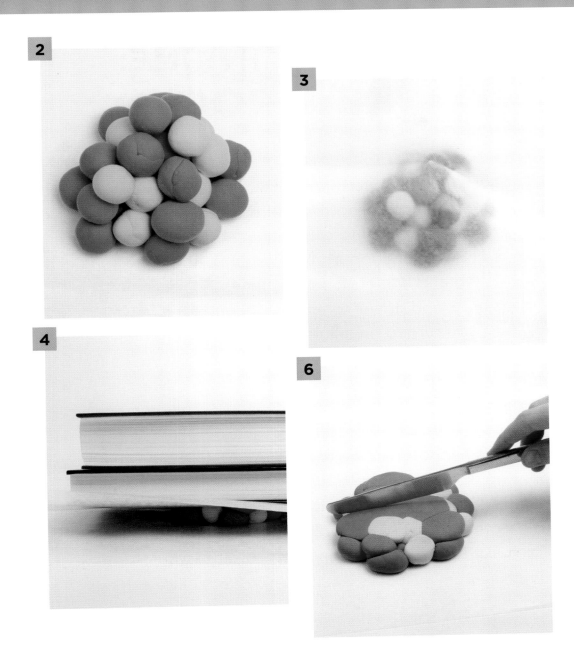

THINKING LIKE A ROCK

Humans have always depended on rocks. We began using stone tools more than 2 million years ago. And, some people even called rock caves home!

Rocks are still used to create shelter. Stones can be used to build houses or support skyscrapers. And, limestone can be crushed and heated to make cement. This is mixed with water, sand, and gravel to make concrete for sidewalks.

Have you turned on a light today? You might have a sedimentary rock called coal to thank! Coal is made from dead plant material that gathered in ancient swamps. Much of it began forming more than 300 million years ago. Today, we burn coal to make electricity.

Rocks cannot become extinct. Yet, Earth is affected by how we collect and use them. For example, coal mining can cause air and water pollution. This can be reduced by using other forms of power. Do you have any other ideas? Think like a rock and imagine long into the future!

Thousands of years ago, people built homes in caves in Arizona. Today, visitors can see these rock homes at Canyon de Chelly ▶ National Monument.

GLOSSARY

collide—to come together with force. An act or instance of colliding is a collision.

dissolve—to cause to pass into solution or become liquid.

element—any of the more than 100 simple substances made of atoms of only one kind.

hot spot—a place where melted rock from beneath Earth's surface melts through the crust to form a volcano.

magma—melted rock beneath Earth's surface.

rapids—a fast-moving part of a river. Rocks or logs often break the surface of the water in this area.

silt—very small bits of rock.

weathering—the breaking down of rock in its original position at or near Earth's surface.

SAYING IT

Carboniferous—kahr-buh-NIH-fuh-ruhs

Cretaceous—krih-TAY-shuhs

igneous—IHG-nee-uhs

Kilauea—kee-lah-WAY-ah

metamorphic—meh-tuh-MAWR-fihk

pumice—PUH-muhs

serpentinite—SUHR-puhn-tee-nite

ONLINE RESOURCES

Booklinks
NONFICTION NETWORK
FREE! ONLINE NONFICTION RESOURCES

To learn more about rocks, please visit **abdobooklinks.com** or scan this QR code. These links are routinely monitored and updated to provide the most current information available.

INDEX